DO NOT REMOVE
CARDS FROM POCKET

D1071372

2/93

DEMCO

SPORTS GREAT
CAL
RIPKEN, JR.

—Sports Great Books—

Sports Great Jim Abbott (ISBN 0-89490-395-0)

Sports Great Charles Barkley (ISBN 0-89490-386-1)

Sports Great Larry Bird (ISBN 0-89490-368-3)

Sports Great Bobby Bonilla (ISBN 0-89490-417-5)

Sports Great Will Clark (ISBN 0-89490-390-X)

Sports Great Roger Clemens (ISBN 0-89490-284-9)

Sports Great John Elway (ISBN 0-89490-282-2)

Sports Great Patrick Ewing (ISBN 0-89490-369-1)

Sports Great Orel Hershiser (ISBN 0-89490-389-6)

Sports Great Bo Jackson (ISBN 0-89490-281-4)

Sports Great Magic Johnson (Revised and Expanded)
(ISBN 0-89490-348-9)

Sports Great Michael Jordan (ISBN 0-89490-370-5)

Sports Great Kevin Mitchell (ISBN 0-89490-388-8)

Sports Great Joe Montana (ISBN 0-89490-371-3)

Sports Great Hakeem Olajuwon (ISBN 0-89490-372-1)

Sports Great Kirby Puckett (ISBN 0-89490-392-6)

Sports Great Cal Ripken, Jr. (ISBN 0-89490-387-X)

Sports Great David Robinson (ISBN 0-89490-373-X)

Sports Great Nolan Ryan (ISBN 0-89490-394-2)

Sports Great Barry Sanders (ISBN 0-89490-418-3)

Sports Great Darryl Strawberry (ISBN 0-89490-291-1)

Sports Great Isiah Thomas (ISBN 0-89490-374-8)

Sports Great Herschel Walker (ISBN 0-89490-207-5)

SPORTS GREAT
CAL
RIPKEN, JR.

Glen Macnow

—Sports Great Books—

ENSLOW PUBLISHERS, INC.

Bloy St. & Ramsey Ave. P.O. Box 38
Box 777   Aldershot
Hillside, N.J. 07205   Hants GU12 6BP
U.S.A.   U.K.

Dedicated to my sons, Ted and Alex,
who make it fun to be a fan again.

Library of Congress Cataloging-in-Publication Data
Macnow, Glen.
  Sports great Cal Ripken, Jr. / Glen Macnow.
      p. cm.— (Sports great books)
  Includes index.
  Summary: A biography of the superstar shortstop for the Baltimore Orioles.
  ISBN 0-89490-387-X
    1. Ripken, Cal, 1960– —Juvenile literature. 2. Baseball
players—United States—Biography—Juvenile literature.
[1. Ripken, Cal, 1960–. 2. Baseball players.] I. Series.
GV865.R47M33 1993
796.357'092—dc20
[B]
                                                    92-24158
                                                        CIP
                                                         AC
Printed in the United States of America

10 9 8 7 6 5 4 3 2 1

Photo Credits: Baltimore Orioles/Jerry Wachter, pp. 9, 11, 13, 17, 19, 21, 23, 27, 30, 32, 35, 37, 39, 41, 45, 47, 49, 51, 55, 57, 59.

Cover Photo: Baltimore Orioles/Jerry Wachter

Contents

Chapter 1

Imagine if you could build the perfect baseball player. What would he be like?

First, he would be strong. He would play every day, even if he had the flu or a sprained ankle. He would never ask to rest during the second game of a doubleheader. He would never want to be taken out for a pinch hitter against a tough pitcher like Nolan Ryan.

Second, he would be a shortstop, because that is the toughest position to play. He would be among the best fielders, bobbling few grounders and gracefully turning the double play. His arm would be strong and true.

Third, he would be a great hitter. Each season his team could count on him for 25 home runs, 35 doubles, and 100 runs batted in. He would play even better when the game was on the line. As he got older, his stroke would become even more powerful.

You could add other qualities to this fantasy ballplayer. Make him loyal, the type who would play forever in one city and never try to leave for more money. Make him polite to fans and reporters. Make him a leader among teammates and liked even by opponents. Make him Rookie of the Year and a two-time Most Valuable Player.

Want to go further? Imagine that this player is the son of a coach and the big brother of the second baseman. That would be the perfect player. He would even be wholesome enough to do commercials for milk. Of course, such a player is too perfect to ever be real. But he is.

Cal Ripken, Jr., is all those things. He is an all-star shortstop for the Baltimore Orioles. He is both a great hitter and a great fielder. He is durable enough to have played 1,735 games in a row by the end of the 1992 season. That's the second-longest streak in major league history. If things go well, Cal should break Lou Gehrig's record in 1995.

Ripken plays on a team where his brother Billy is the second baseman. His father, Cal, Sr., once managed the club and is now the third-base coach. "When we were boys, Billy and I would pretend we were grownups playing together in the major leagues," Cal says. "I think all brothers pretend that way. But in our case, the dream came true."

In many ways, Ripken is a baseball fan's dream come true. At six feet four and 220 pounds, he is the biggest shortstop in major league history. Still, his defense is so steady that he would be considered a star player even if he hit just .240 every year.

In 1990, for example, Cal set a major-league record by making just three errors in a whole season. How good is that? Consider that Brooks Robinson—the best-fielding third baseman ever—once made three errors in one inning. Robinson, by the way, was Cal's hero as a child.

As good as Ripken's fielding is, his hitting is even better. He is the only shortstop ever to hit 20 or more home runs in 10 straight seasons. In 1991—the year in which he won his

Cal is one of the best-hitting shortstops in major league history.

second Most Valuable Player Award—Cal piled up a .323 batting average, 46 doubles, 34 homers, and 114 runs batted in.

"I never saw some of the old-timers," said the Detroit Tigers' manager, Sparky Anderson. "But in all my 57 years, Ripken is the best shortstop I've ever seen. He's the complete package."

Is Cal the top shortstop ever? That's difficult to say. Baseball historians usually call Honus Wagner the best. Wagner played twenty-one seasons, mostly for the Pittsburgh Pirates. He was a fluid fielder, and his .329 lifetime batting average is among the highest ever. But Wagner's career ended in 1917. Few alive today ever saw him play and can compare him to Ripken.

More recently, Ernie Banks of the Chicago Cubs was called the best. Banks played from 1953 to 1971. He twice led the National League in home runs. Like Cal, he was twice named the Most Valuable Player. But Banks was never strong on defense. After eight seasons at shortstop, he was moved to first base for the rest of his career.

Certainly, no one can argue that Ripken is the top shortstop of the past thirty years. No shortstop comes close to his record of starting in eight straight All-Star games.

Despite it all, Ripken gets noticed much less than most major-league superstars. Others make headlines for complaining about their contracts or abusing drugs or arguing with umpires. But Cal only draws notice for his good play. And playing in Baltimore, he does not get the attention he would in a larger city such as New York or Los Angeles or Chicago.

For one week in 1991, however, Ripken took baseball's center stage. As usual, Cal was voted by fans to be the American League's starting shortstop in the All-Star game. He

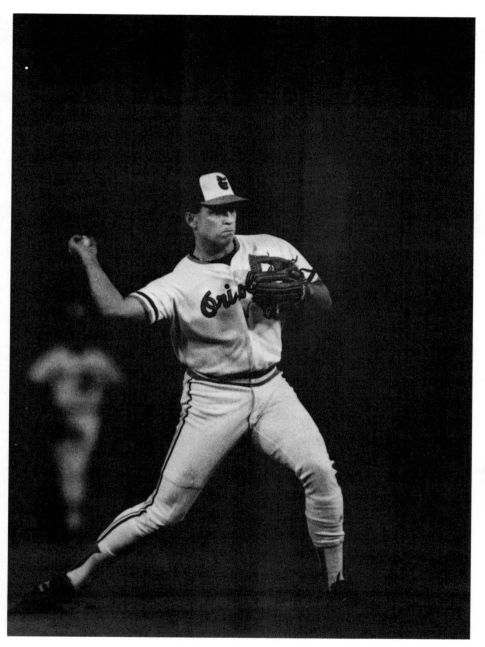

Cal's sure hands and strong arm make him a great defensive player.

came to the game, in Toronto, leading the league in batting and second in home runs.

The day before the All-Star game, some of baseball's top sluggers gathered at the Toronto SkyDome for a homer-hitting contest. Will Clark of the San Francisco Giants was there. So was Howard Johnson of the New York Mets. Many thought that Darryl Strawberry of the Los Angeles Dodgers would win the home-run derby. Or perhaps Cecil Fielder, the gigantic belter for the Detroit Tigers.

In all, there were eight players in the contest, including Cal. The seven other men took 85 swings against batting-practice pitching. They combined for 15 homers.

Ripken took 22 swings. He hit an astonishing 12 homers, some of them way into the upper decks.

One of Cal's blasts nearly hit a hot dog vendor in the stands 440 feet away. Almost before that ball landed, another shot went 450 feet into the third deck. On his last swing, Ripken decided to dig down deep. He hit the longest ball of his life. It was a 475-foot belt that might have gone farther had a brave fan not reached up to stop it. The ball fell in the fifth deck at the SkyDome. Only Jose Canseco had reached that deck before.

The other players could hardly believe Cal's performance. "I've never done anything close to that," said Chicago White Sox catcher Carlton Fisk. "In fact, I've never seen another player do anything like that."

Ripken continued his super performance during the All-Star game the next night. In the first inning, he whacked a single off of Tom Glavine, the National League's starting pitcher. Then, in the third, he came up against Dennis Martinez, the tough curveball specialist.

American League stars Rickey Henderson and Wade Boggs were already on base when Ripken came to bat.

Ripken in his familiar home run trot. He hit 20 or more homers for 10 straight seasons.

Martinez threw two low pitches for balls, then a called strike. On the next pitch, he hung a slider, and Ripken jumped at it. The ball exploded off of Cal's bat. It sailed over the left-field wall as 52,000 fans cheered.

Ripken's home run gave his side a 3-1 lead. The American League went on to win, 4-2. Cal was chosen as the game's Most Valuable Player.

Late in the game, Ripken was due to bat against Rob Dibble, the Cincinnati Reds' hard-throwing relief pitcher. But American League manager Tony LaRussa said he wanted to give each All-Star a chance to play. So he pinch-hit Ozzie Guillen for Ripken.

Cal made it clear that he would have liked to stay in the game. But he did not complain.

"Dibble throws the ball a hundred miles an hour," Ripken said. "I was looking forward to the challenge. But I understand that Ozzie is here to play, too. I had no problem sitting down."

Other players might have complained about being pulled after hitting a home run, but not Cal. In his mind, there is nothing to be gained by moaning. He always tries to lead by example—both on and off the field.

That, he explains, comes easily. After all, it is the way he was brought up.

Chapter 2

Many boys learn how to hit a baseball by batting against their fathers. Cal Ripken, Jr., was no different. Except that young Cal did not take his swings in the backyard or local park. He took them at real baseball stadiums all across the country.

Cal's dad, Cal Ripken, Sr., started out as a minor-league catcher for the Baltimore Orioles. But in 1960, the year Cal was born, Mr. Ripken hurt his shoulder. He could no longer throw well. So the club offered him a job as a minor-league manager.

For the next fifteen years, Mr. Ripken moved from town to town while working for the Orioles. There were eighteen stops in all—from Leesburg, Florida, to Appleton, Wisconsin, to Elmira, New York, to Dallas, Texas. During the school year, young Cal, his brothers and sister, and his mom stayed at their home in Aberdeen, Maryland. But when the summer started, they loaded up a trailer and moved to wherever Mr. Ripken was managing.

The travel was both fun and tough for the Ripken kids. They had to leave their friends behind each summer and make new friends. Mostly, they were pals with one another. Cal, the oldest, recalls how he used to fight with his brothers Fred and Billy and his sister Ellen. But they would make up and invent games by the hour. Baseball was always the biggest part of their lives. They talked about it at the dinner table and on long car rides. Even the bedtime stories Mr. Ripken told his children usually had to do with baseball.

The best part for Cal was watching his dad teach young players. Even as a little boy, he thirsted for a locker of his own. He spent summers hanging around the locker room, wearing a miniature Orioles uniform, and getting baseball tips from all the players. Years later, when he became a superstar, Cal realized how well that time had paid off. He said, "I got to learn the game from people who really knew it. Most kids don't get the chance to watch real players every day."

Sometimes, Mr. Ripken would take Cal and his brothers onto the field for batting practice. Even when Cal was young, his dad would throw curve balls and fast balls, knuckleballs and sliders. Soon, Cal became able to hit each pitch. At twelve, he hit his first ball out of the park. At thirteen, he put on his dad's big catcher's mitt and started catching 80-mile-per-hour fastballs from minor-league pitchers.

Mr. Ripken did not want to push his sons into playing baseball. It was his job and he loved it, he explained. But he wanted the boys to do whatever they enjoyed. Fred, the middle brother, gave up the sport at age nine because he did not like practicing. But Cal and Billy loved it. They couldn't get enough. Cal later described it as a kind of hunger that he always needed to feed.

As much as Mr. Ripken wanted to help, his job kept him too busy to spend a lot of time coaching his sons. So Cal's mom, Violet Ripken, took over. She knew baseball from all her years with Cal's dad. She knew when Cal's batting stance

Cal learned his baseball lessons from his dad, a former minor-league player.

was out of whack or when he was holding his glove wrong in the field. Years later, Cal would remember a Little League game he pitched when he was eleven. It was 30 degrees, and the wind was so strong that he was blown off the mound. The stands were empty except for one woman with an Orioles' cap pulled down over her ears. It was his mom.

When Cal was fifteen, his dad became a coach with the Orioles in Baltimore. Then Cal had a chance to see the sport's greatest players up close. He used to sit around the team's clubhouse and listen to men like Al Bumbry, Bobby Grich, and Doug DeCinces talk about details of the game. He took pitching lessons from Hall of Famer Jim Palmer.

On weekends, Cal and Billy would come to Baltimore's Memorial Stadium early. They would shag flies in the outfield, take batting practice from real major-league pitchers, and work as batboys during the game. On week nights, Cal would arrive at the ballpark around the fifth inning, after playing in his own high school game. In fact, he would still be wearing his dirty uniform. The stadium ticket-takers knew who he was and let him in for free.

These days Ripken is famous as a great shortstop. But he first was noticed by pro scouts as a pitcher. Cal liked pitching best because it put him in the middle of the action and in control of every play. At Aberdeen High School outside of Baltimore, he was the school's star hurler. All those private lessons from Palmer were paying off. Cal's fastball was not great, but he almost never walked batters. As a high school senior, he won seven games, lost just two, and allowed fewer than one run a game.

In games he wasn't pitching, Cal played shortstop. In his last year of high school, he batted .492 with 29 RBIs in just 20 games.

The major-league scouts began coming to watch his

Even as little boys, Cal and Billy Ripken dreamed of playing together in the majors.

games. Many thought that he could make it to the majors as either a pitcher or a shortstop. Several clubs said they were interested in drafting him. Cal, of course, hoped he would end up with the Orioles. And why not? He had grown up around the team. His friends were there. So was his father.

Cal got his wish. The Orioles picked him in the second round of the 1978 draft. There was just one question left: What position would he play? Cal and the club's coaches agreed that he would be more valuable playing every day, rather than pitching once every five days. From that point on, he played only in the infield.

That summer, when he was just seventeen, Cal went to play for the Bluefield Orioles of the Appalachian Rookie League. Living away from home was a tough adjustment. But Cal had prepared his whole life for pro ball. He was ready. In 63 games he batted just .264 and was too skinny to hit any homers, but he was chosen the league's best fielder by its managers.

The next season, Cal was promoted to Single-A Miami and then Double-A Charlotte. He began to bulk up, and his hitting improved. In 1980, he played the whole year at Charlotte. He smashed 25 homers and was named to the Southern League's All-Star team.

Ripken started the 1981 season at Triple-A Rochester—one step away from the major leagues. He dominated the league's pitchers so much that the Orioles could no longer keep him down in the farm system. That September, they called him up to the big leagues.

Until then, everything had come easily for Cal. But major-league pitchers threw a little bit harder than what he was used to. Major-league fielders got to some of his balls that would have fallen through for hits in the minors. In 23 games

Cal as a rookie with the Orioles in 1982.

with the Orioles that fall, Cal batted just .128 with no home runs.

Cal began to worry whether he was good enough to make it. Years later he said, "There's always a point where you question if you can do it in the majors, even if you've done it in the minors. I was beginning to wonder whether the Orioles would stick with me." Rather than just worry, Cal spent that off-season working harder than ever. He lifted weights to improve his strength. He took batting practice every day. And he asked his father for help. In this case, the talk wasn't father to son; it was coach to player. Before the 1982 season, the Orioles traded third baseman Doug DeCinces. They told Cal he would shift back and forth between shortstop and third base. Cal said he was ready.

But he wasn't. Through the first 25 games, he was hitting just .117. Some fans and writers began to say that he was on the club only because his father was a coach. And the more that manager Earl Weaver kept telling Cal that things would improve, the more the twenty-one-year-old began to worry he would be a permanent flop. Then, during a game in May, Reggie Jackson of the California Angels pulled Ripken aside during a break in the action. Jackson was a superstar who had gone through tough times early in his career. He had some advice.

"Hey, kid," Jackson said. "You're pressing too hard. Don't try to be Babe Ruth. Just be yourself. Do what Cal Ripken can do."

The words clicked in Cal's mind. They jolted him into realizing that he had been putting too much pressure on himself to become an immediate star. The next day, feeling more relaxed at the plate, he got two hits. From the dugout, Jackson gave him the thumbs-up sign. The day after that, Cal had two more hits.

Ripken was voted the American League's Rookie of the Year in 1982 after bashing 28 home runs.

From that point on, Ripken was unstoppable. At season's end, he led all first-year players with 28 homers and 93 RBIs. He raised his batting average to .264—a long way from what it had been in early May. And he played in 160 of the club's 162 games, an early sign of his toughness.

The newspaper writers who cover the American League rewarded Cal by voting him Rookie of the Year, ahead of Kent Hrbek of the Minnesota Twins and Wade Boggs of the Boston Red Sox. Ripken, as usual, was modest when he got the award. "My manager and my teammates really deserve it," he said. "They stuck with me when I wasn't doing the job."

Now, he said, the goal was to get the Orioles to a World Series.

Chapter 3

During a great athlete's career, the time usually comes when fans suddenly say: This is a superstar. It might occur when the player leads his team to a championship. Or it might come during a season in which the player proves that he is among the best in his sport.

For Cal Ripken, the moment came in 1983. At the young age of twenty-three, Cal led the Orioles to a World Series victory. He was also chosen the American League's Most Valuable Player for batting .318 and leading the league in doubles, runs, and hits. And he played in every inning of every game, starting an amazing streak that would run for many seasons.

Suddenly, people began to realize that Cal wasn't just a promising young ballplayer. He was the best in the business.

"I don't think I've ever seen a player who was so good at such a young age," said Brooks Robinson, the Hall of Fame third baseman. Robinson said he was glad that the Orioles finally decided to keep Ripken at shortstop because "I didn't want to be known as the second-best third baseman the Orioles ever had."

Ripken's 1983 season was so good that it seemed make-believe. In just his first full season at shortstop, he quickly became the league's top fielder. He learned to move quickly to his left and his right, to charge slow-hit grounders, and to turn on the double play. His powerful throws seemed like they came from a rocket launcher.

Because he is so tall, Cal is not as flashy as many shortstops who play the game. His dives and twirls rarely make the highlight films. But he is a smart player. He always seems to be right where the ball is hit, and the reason has nothing to do with luck. That comes from years of studying where each batter is likely to hit the ball. That allows Cal to position himself in the right spot.

Ripken's big size helps him in other areas. Most smaller shortstops are slap hitters. They rarely rank among the top hitters. They almost never belt home runs. But Cal, because of his strength, quickly became one of the American League's most-feared sluggers. He smacked 27 homers in 1983. In fact, Cal hit more than 20 home runs in each of his first ten seasons.

The way to hit home runs, Ripken once said, is not to try to hit them. In other words, if you aim for a homer, chances are you'll fall short. But if you just try to hit the ball, the home runs will follow.

The 1983 Orioles were one of the best teams of the decade. Their strength was their pitching staff, which featured Scott McGregor, Storm Davis, Mike Boddicker, and Dennis Martinez. There were two star batters—Cal and first baseman Eddie Murray. In fact, Murray finished right behind Ripken in the MVP voting. He and Cal were best friends on the team.

The Orioles won 98 games that season to take the

Cal as a rookie with the Orioles in 1982.

American League East. They had no problem whipping the Chicago White Sox in the play-offs, winning that series three games to one. Cal batted .400 for the series, scoring five runs and driving in two. He was in a groove. Every ball off his bat seemed to fall for a hit. Every time he jumped, the ball ended up in his glove. The game, he told an interviewer after the play-offs, seemed easy.

In the World Series, however, things quickly got more difficult. The Orioles faced the National League champion Philadelphia Phillies, who had star pitchers Steve Carlton and John Denny. Cal's bat suddenly got cold. He managed just three singles in 18 at bats during the series. He had no doubles, no homers, and just one RBI. His fielding continued to be great. But Cal worried that he was letting down his teammates.

He wasn't. As tough as the Phillies' pitchers were, the Orioles' pitchers were better. In five games, they allowed the Phils to score just nine runs. The Orioles won the World Series, four games to one. Now Cal was a Most Valuable Player and a member of the championship team. He and his teammates celebrated by driving in a ticker-tape parade through downtown Baltimore. Things don't get much better than that.

Cal won other awards after the 1983 season. He seemed the favorite of every group voting for a player of the year. There were two reasons. First, of course, was his outstanding performance on the field. Second was the way Cal handled himself off the field. Unlike some players, he loves being a role model for children. So he tries to be the best person he can in order to set a good example.

"Kids look up to athletes," he said. "I know I did when I was young. If a kid playing ball in the backyard wants to pretend to be Cal Ripken, Jr., when he's swinging the bat, I want to be a good role model for him. I don't want to do anything wrong to ruin that image."

To set a good example, Cal helped set up a program called "Don't Start Smoking." It is aimed at convincing teenagers to stay off cigarettes. He has been active in many charities in Baltimore. And he gives speeches warning children to keep away from drugs. "I've never had the urge to try drugs," he said, "because I believe they can harm your body."

In fact, Ripken takes such good care of himself that teammates say they have never even seen him eat a candy bar. He practices and exercises as hard as anyone on the Orioles. His body is 225 pounds of pure muscle. That dedication to hard work has helped Cal stay at the top of his game.

Many athletes are unable to remain stars for a long time. Sometimes their opponents adjust and catch up with them. Other times, they get fat and lazy from too much success. They lose the ambition that made them stars in the first place.

But Ripken is too talented to be stopped by the other team. And he is too devoted to start giving anything less than his best effort. Even as a rookie, he used to say that his goal was to have a long career, to play in the majors for at least fifteen years. No one does that without always giving 100 percent.

That dedication showed in 1984. Many fans wondered whether Cal's MVP season would be a fluke. Would he be able to follow it up with another solid year? Their doubts were quickly removed. Ripken came back to hit .304 and again hit 27 home runs. He also set an American League record for assists by a shortstop by throwing out 583 base runners. The year turned out to be as good as the last one.

In fact, every season during the first part of Ripken's career seemed almost identical. Look at his season-by-season home run marks for six years starting in 1982: 28, 27, 27, 26, 25, 27. That's as consistent as a player can get. From 1983

Ripken loves to meet with kids and help his community.

through 1986, he averaged .296 with 109 runs scored and 95 runs batted in.

Plus, Cal played not just in every game. He played every inning of every game. From June 5, 1982, until September 14, 1987, Ripken never sat down for a pinch hitter or defensive replacement. He totaled 8,243 innings in a row. That is a major-league record that no one ever figures to challenge.

His toughness shows not just in durability, but also in Ripken's approach to baseball. One time, in 1983, White Sox pitcher Rich Dotson wanted to get Ripken to stop crowding home plate. Dotson threw an inside fastball that drilled Cal in the ribs. Cal refused to show that he was hurt by rubbing the bruise. And when he got to first base, he shouted at Dotson, "Is that as hard as you can throw?" The next time he faced Dotson, Ripken got even in another way. He slammed a double.

By the mid-80s, there were no more debates on who was baseball's best shortstop. It was the tall home-run hitter from Baltimore. Other shortstops had great seasons, like Ozzie Smith of the St. Louis Cardinals, Alan Trammell of the Detroit Tigers, and Tony Fernandez of the Toronto Blue Jays. But Ripken had a great season every single year. Baseball's fans recognized this achievement. For eight seasons in a row, starting in 1984, they voted Cal the starting American League shortstop in the All-Star game.

As steady as Ripken was, the Orioles were getting worse around him. After winning the World Series in 1983, they slipped to 85 wins in 1984, then to 83 in 1985. In 1986, Baltimore had its first losing season in nineteen years, winning just 73 games and losing 89. Clearly, changes had to be made.

The first change was the manager. Earl Weaver, who had led the Orioles for seventeen seasons, decided to retire.

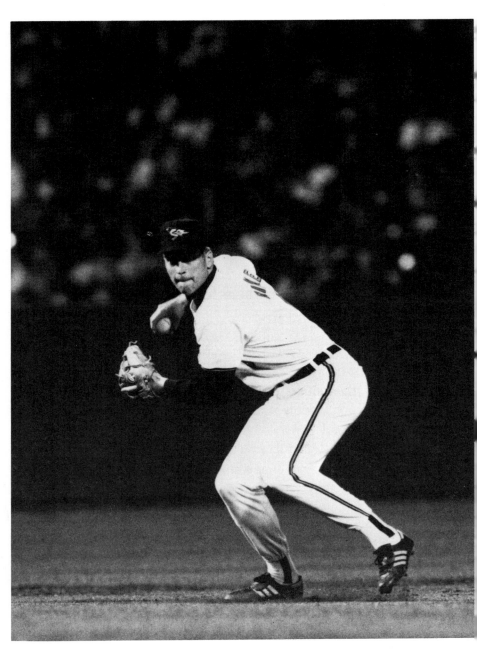

Ripken is such a tough player that he hasn't missed a game in an entire decade.

Weaver was one of the all-time greats. Replacing him would not be easy. But the Orioles had a good candidate whom they had already prepared to take the job. He had spent many seasons as the third-base coach. His name was Cal Ripken, Sr.—Cal's dad.

Baltimore also needed to change some of its players. A few had gotten old and were no longer very good. A few others did not turn out to be as talented as the Orioles had expected. So the club made a lot of trades heading into the 1987 season. One position they did not trade for, of course, was shortstop. Another was second base. The Orioles needed a new player at second. But they thought they had a good one ready to come up from their minor-league team. His name was Billy Ripken—Cal's brother.

"I don't know how well we will do next season," Cal told reporters after his father was hired to manage the club. "But I'll tell you one thing. It's sure going to be interesting."

Chapter 4

Remember how Mr. Ripken had pitched batting practice to his sons when they were growing up? At the time, Cal and Billy liked to pretend that they were teammates in the big leagues. Of course, they figured it was just a dream.

But the dream came true in 1987. When Mr. Ripken became the Orioles' manager, one of his first moves was to bring Billy up from the minor leagues. Cal would play shortstop, and Billy would play second base, just a few feet away. It was the first time in major-league history that a manager had two of his sons on the same team. It was also the first time that Cal and Billy had played on the same ball club since they were children.

Cal loved being around his family. After all, how many other grown men get to visit the same cities, wear the same uniform, and go to work every day with their brother and dad? One of the toughest parts of being a pro athlete is that you are away from home so often while playing in other cities. It sure gets easier when some of your family travels with you.

Still, Mr. Ripken was careful not to give his sons any

In 1987, the Ripkens' dream came true. Cal and Billy got to play for a team managed by their father.

special treatment. He didn't want other players thinking that he favored his own sons. One of his rules was that, around the ballpark, the brothers did not call him "Dad" and he did not call them "Son." And when Billy went into a bad hitting slump during the 1987 season, Mr. Ripken benched him for a while—just as he would another player.

When they were boys, Cal and Billy competed against each other in everything. The brothers would play Ping-Pong for hours. They would shoot marbles until one owned all the other's best glassies. Sometimes, they would just sit in their bedroom and take turns tossing a balled-up sock into a trash can. The point was not just to see which brother was better at something. It was also to keep practicing so they both could improve.

In baseball, however, Cal has always been the better player. Billy, who is four years younger, will never be a superstar. He is not a top hitter like his big brother. He almost never hits home runs. "Cal is a great player," Billy once said. "I just want people to call me a good player. I think I can do that if I follow Cal's advice. He told me that you've got to work your tail off all the time to make it in this game. You can't ever be satisfied."

What Billy is best at is fielding. Like Cal, he is one of the smoothest glove men at his position. How come? Billy says it comes from years of having their dad hit ground balls to all the players during infield practice. "Dad always hit them harder to us than to anyone else," Billy says. "We had to learn to handle the tough ones."

They certainly learned well. In 1990, the two brothers set a major-league record for fewest errors—11—by a shortstop-second baseman combination. Billy made just eight errors. Cal made just three. All those years of practicing together as kids seemed to

With Cal and Billy playing up the middle, the Orioles can boast of having the best defense in baseball.

pay off. Now each brother always seems to know where the other is going to be on every play.

In many ways, that 1987 season seemed perfect to Cal. He could stand on the field and look over at his brother playing second base. Meanwhile, his buddy, Eddie Murray, was playing first base. And his boss was his dad. What could be better?

While father and son were all business during the games, they were good friends afterward. Most nights they would stay at the ballpark until late at night. All the other players would have gone home. But Cal and his dad would stay to talk about at bats, plays, or pitchers—anything interesting that happened during that day's game.

In fact, Cal and his dad are such good friends that, when Cal got married in 1987, he had Mr. Ripken serve as his best man. Billy was an usher at the wedding. Today Cal and his wife, Kelly, have a daughter named Rachel.

In other ways, though, 1987 was not a good year for Cal or the rest of the Orioles. The team did not play any better for Mr. Ripken than it had under Earl Weaver. The Orioles won just 67 games while losing 95. Some of their players were injured. Some of their trades did not work out well. A few of their veteran players seemed to lose interest in the season.

Sometimes, players on losing teams get down and stop giving their best. But not Cal. As usual, he played every game, every inning. As usual, he hit 27 home runs and drove in 98 runs. His batting average was just .252, the worst since his first few games in 1981. But part of the reason for that was that opposing pitchers were no longer giving him good pitches to hit. They would rather pitch to his teammates.

Things did not get any better for the Orioles in 1988. In April, the team started the season by losing the first six games. It was clear that changes had to be made. The first change was

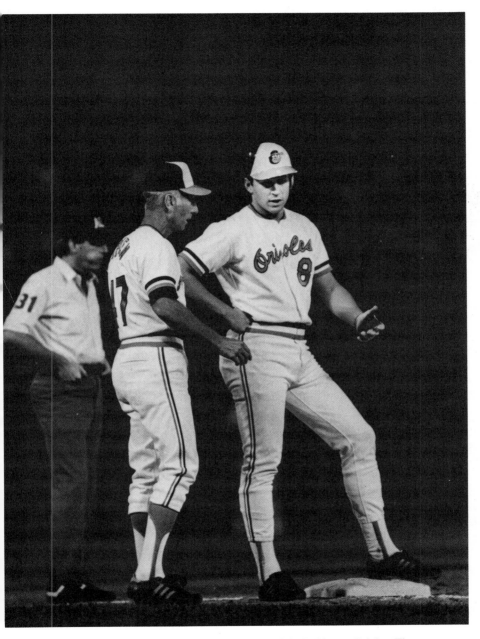

Cal and his father are much more than members of the Baltimore Orioles. They are also best friends.

a tough one. The team's owner and general manager removed Cal Ripken, Sr., as the Orioles' manager.

In baseball, as in all sports, managers and coaches get replaced whenever a team is playing poorly. The old joke is that the manager never really owns his job. Instead, he just borrows it for a while. Still, when Mr. Ripken left, it was heartbreaking for Cal and Billy. They had seen their lifelong dream come true. Now, after little more than one year, it was ending. Cal understood that these things happen in baseball. And he knew that his job was to keep going out every day and giving his best effort. Still, it was tough. At the time, Cal said, "I just have to block my personal feelings out of my mind. I just have to keep playing to win. I have to act like a professional."

Mr. Ripken stayed with the Orioles, returning to his old job as third base coach. The new manager was Frank Robinson, a Hall of Fame outfielder who had starred for Baltimore in the 1960s. Robinson said his goal was to quickly turn the club around.

However, that was easier said than done. The Orioles lost their first game under Robinson, dropping them to 0-7 for the season. Then they lost their next game. And the next. By the middle of April, they had won no games and lost 12. Now, they were about to leave Baltimore for a two-week road trip. One more loss would tie an 84-year-old record for the worst start ever by a major-league team.

Ripken wanted no part of this kind of record. Before the first road game against the Milwaukee Brewers, Ripken and Robinson called the Orioles together for a meeting. What could they do to win, they asked the players. No one had an answer. Certainly, they had all been trying hard. But maybe, everyone agreed, they could try a little harder.

It didn't help. The Orioles lost game 13, and then another,

and then another. By the end of April, they had lost 21 straight games. It seemed to some that they might never win again.

Then, on April 29, 1988, they finally won. Eddie Murray hit a first-inning homer. Cal had four hits and scored three runs. The Orioles beat the Chicago White Sox 9-0 to end the worst stretch of baseball in their history.

After the season, a writer asked Ripken how bad he had felt during the losing streak.

"Nothing can be worse than this," Cal said. "But we can learn from this. No matter what happens in the future, we can say, 'We'll handle this. It can't be as bad as what happened in 1988.' We will all be stronger for it."

For several seasons, Cal and Eddie Murray gave the Orioles a double threat of home run hitters.

The Orioles won just 55 games and lost 107 in 1988. They finished in last place. Some fans worried that Cal might not enjoy being a great player on a bad team. They wondered if he would leave the club to sign with another when his contract was finished.

But Ripken had no such ideas. From the time he had been a little boy, the only team he wanted to play for was the Orioles. And like his hero, Brooks Robinson, he wanted to spend his entire career with one team. So in July of 1988, not long after his father was replaced as manager, Ripken signed a new contract with the Orioles. It was a magnificent deal. Cal would earn $2.45 million a year for three seasons. Suddenly, he was one of the best-paid players in all of sports. That only seemed fair, since he is one of the top athletes around.

The money was great, Cal said. But staying in Baltimore was the most important thing. After the Orioles' terrible season, he wanted to be there when the team turned things around. Cal told reporters, "I started a job when I came here in 1981. The job is far from being finished. So I'm staying in Baltimore. I've got work to do."

Chapter 5

Imagine not missing a day of school in ten years. Imagine having a job and not calling in sick for 1,735 days in a row. It seems impossible. After all, everyone gets the flu once in a while. Everyone who works needs an occasional day off to rest or play. But not Cal Ripken. For every day of the baseball season since May 30, 1982, Ripken's name has been written into the Orioles' starting lineup. At the end of 1992, he had started 1,735 games in a row. In fact, at one point, Cal played every inning of every game for almost six full years. Of all Cal's deeds, some people think "The Streak" is his greatest accomplishment.

Sure, baseball is fun. But for the men who play it for a living, it is also hard work. Players can get hurt by sliding, by getting hit by a pitch, or just by running. Even those who don't get injured find themselves too tired to play on occasion. Or they just need to rest their minds.

But not Cal Ripken. One of his teammates, first baseman Randy Milligan, said, "Every player has days when he's not feeling so good. I have them all the time. But I've never heard

Cal say he doesn't feel well. All he ever says is, 'I'm ready. When does the game start?'"

Only once in ten years has Ripken come close to missing a game. It happened on the second day of the 1985 season, against the Texas Rangers. Ripken, running the bases, got the spikes of his shoes stuck on second base. As he tried to lift his foot, his ankle twisted, and he fell down. Soon, his ankle swelled up like a balloon.

The Orioles had the next day off, so Cal stayed in bed. The following afternoon, no one expected him to play. But there he was, taking batting practice before the game. He winced in pain as he swung the bat. But he played anyway. "I want to be in the thick of things," Cal said. "I always want to play. I never want to watch." If Cal continues to play every game, he will break the great Lou Gehrig's record of 2,130 straight games sometime in June 1995. Until Cal came along, baseball experts said Gehrig's mark was one that would never be topped. In fact, Gehrig earned the nickname "The Iron Horse" by playing so many games in a row. Cal is still a long way from Gehrig's record. But no one is betting these days against his breaking it.

One reason is that Ripken never gets tired of baseball. He never stops trying to get better. Johnny Oates, who managed the Orioles in 1991, said that Cal has not even missed infield practice or batting practice in ten years. One time in 1991, after going without a hit for two games, Cal came to the ballpark two hours early for extra hitting practice.

That kind of desire impresses his teammates. Cal knows that the only way to keep his streak going and remain one of baseball's top stars is to keep working and exercising. He likes to wear a T-shirt in the clubhouse that says, "Fat Birds Don't Fly." It means that Orioles who don't stay in shape are not going to succeed.

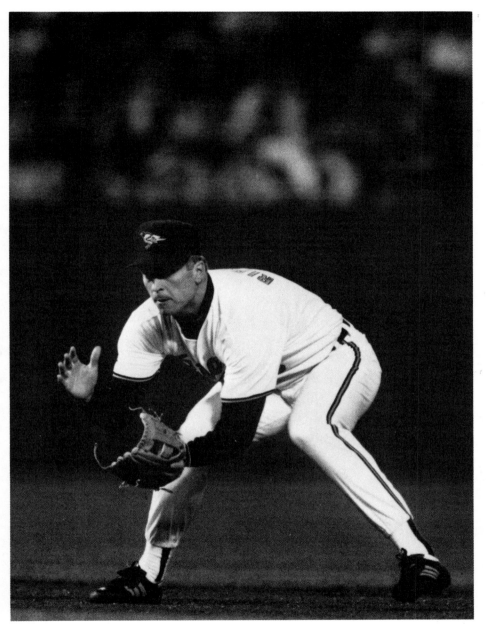

Even though he plays hard every day, Ripken has been able to avoid injuries throughout his career.

Every day, Ripken does his sit-ups, push-ups, and pull-ups. In the winter, when there is no baseball, he plays pick-up basketball games or swims 100 laps across a pool. Instead of tiring him out, the extra work builds up his strength.

After the Orioles' disastrous 1988 season, the club made many changes. One was trading first baseman Eddie Murray, Cal's friend and the team's only other slugger. Manager Frank Robinson decided to bring up young players from the minors to see how they would do. No one expected much. But the Orioles played surprisingly well. They won 87 games, lost 75, and finished second in the American League East. Ripken, as usual, was the key player. And now, at age twenty-nine, he was one of the veteran leaders on the club.

Mostly, Cal has always led by example. Off the field, he never rips the manager or umpires. He doesn't complain about his salary. He doesn't treat people rudely.

On the field, Cal makes the most of what he has. He isn't as fast as Rickey Henderson. He doesn't have Jose Canseco's swing, or Shawon Dunston's great arm. Nor does he have Ozzie Smith's ability to get to the ball. "He just finds ways to beat the other guy," said Frank Robinson. "When the game is on the line, he finds the way to win. Part of it is that he's so smart and studies the game so hard."

How smart? Here's one example. Late in the 1989 season, Robinson decided to put in rookie pitcher Ben McDonald for the first time. McDonald entered in the middle of the game, and he was nervous. There were runners on first and third base and a dangerous hitter at the plate. What a tough way for a rookie to break in!

Cal, seeing how scared the young pitcher was, called time out and trotted to the mound to calm him down. Cal had seen

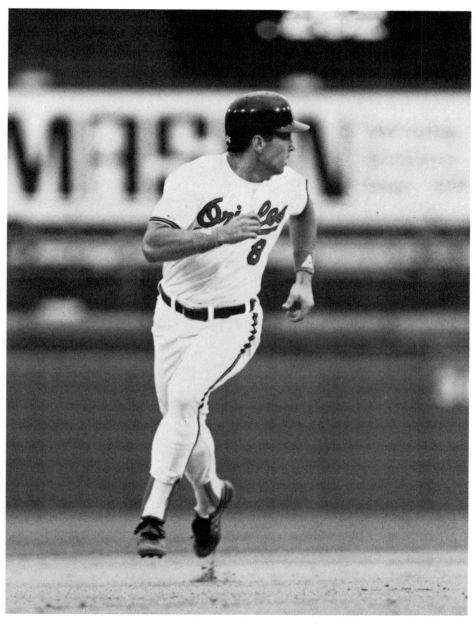

Cal is always a heads-up player—whether he is batting, fielding, or running the bases.

McDonald pitch in the minors. He knew that McDonald had been called for several balks. So Cal reminded McDonald to come to a complete stop. Then he said, "Just throw strikes, Ben. If they hit the ball, we'll get the outs for you. That's what we're here for."

McDonald's first pitch was over the plate. The batter, Cory Snyder, hit a slow two-hopper back up the middle. Ripken had studied Snyder before and knew where he usually hit the ball. So Cal was standing exactly in the right spot. He caught the ball easily and flipped it to his brother at second base to start a double play. McDonald had thrown his first major-league pitch and gotten two men out—thanks to Ripken.

Because Cal is such an excellent hitter, people sometimes don't notice his fielding. But he is one of the best. He has led the American League more than twenty times in different defensive categories. Back in 1984, he had set the league record by throwing out 584 runners. But, in 1990, he set an even more impressive mark. In 161 games, he made just three errors. That broke the old record, which was six. Imagine handling 680 chances for the season and bobbling just three!

Cal is not as flashy a fielder as some of baseball's other top shortstops. With his big size, he can't dive around as quickly as they do. Instead, he plays a style that is best described as "steady." He has big, soft hands that have been trained not to bobble balls. And, as the episode with Ben McDonald shows, he knows where to play the hitters. All those years of growing up around the clubhouse helped him learn the importance of that knowledge.

"The first rule of baseball is to catch the ball," Ripken says. "Then you have to know what to do with it after you catch it. A shortstop has to be prepared. You have to know the hitters. How do they hit with two strikes? How they hit with two balls? How do they adjust to each pitcher?"

That's a lot to learn, and it can only be learned by playing baseball—and studying it—day after day, year after year. And, certainly, Cal Ripken has done that.

Shortstop is baseball's most demanding position. The shortstop must be able to field hot grounders. He must have an arm strong enough to throw out runners from deep in the hole. And he must be quick enough to pivot, leap, and throw on the double play. For those reasons, it is also the most exhausting position.

Therefore, it is more amazing that Ripken has not missed a game in close to ten seasons. But by the middle of 1989, some fans and teammates began to wonder: Was Cal hurting his game by playing every day?

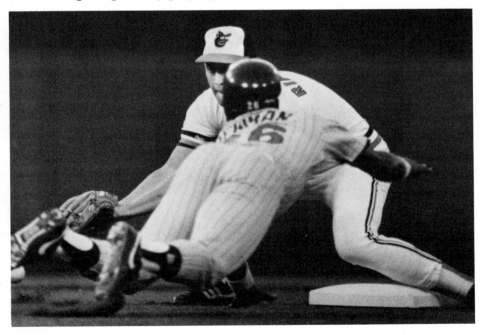

Shortstop is baseball's toughest position, but Cal is up to the task.

The questions began when Cal's batting statistics began to go down. Early in his career, he regularly batted over .300. But in 1989, he hit just .257. His home-run totals also dropped—from 27 in 1987, to 23 in 1988, to a career-low 21 in 1989.

Ripken said the problem was that he was trying too hard. After Murray's trade, Cal was the Orioles' only slugger. So he was attempting to do it all himself. He stopped taking walks and began to swing at more bad pitches. The result was more outs. The solution, Ripken said, was to go back to his old batting style.

But others viewed it differently. Many said he looked tired. They said the demand of playing every game had taken too much out of him. They suggested that he take a rest.

Cal refused. "It used to bother me when people said I was hurting myself and hurting the team by playing every day," he said. "But I know I'm not. The least I can do is come out and play every day." Still, Cal knew inside that his hitting was getting worse. He realized it was time to make changes. After ten years of taking batting advice only from his father, Cal decided to seek someone else's opinion. Midway through the 1990 season, with his batting average down at .209, Cal went to Frank Robinson for help. This was a wise choice. Robinson is a Hall of Famer and one of the top home-run hitters in baseball history.

Robinson told Cal how he once went 22 at bats without a hit. Even the best ballplayers go through slumps, he said. After talking it over, the two men worked together in the batting cage. They came up with a new batting stance for Cal and a new approach. He would no longer chase bad pitches.

Cal's hitting improved immediately. His batting average

Ripken has a classic batting stance that adds to his power.

rose to .250 by the end of the season. It was the lowest average of his career, but a lot better than the .209 he had been hitting earlier. After nine full seasons in the majors, Cal found himself looking forward to 1991 with the eagerness of a rookie. With his new approach, he predicted he would play as well as he had in his younger days.

Cal was wrong. He played a lot better.

Chapter 6

During the winter before the 1991 season, Ripken and Robinson continued to tinker with Cal's batting style. Cal built a batting cage with a mechanical pitcher in his backyard so that he could practice for hours every day. Here was a thirty-year-old veteran working with the dedication of a nineteen-year-old prospect.

Why? Because Cal could not stand having people regard him as less than the best in the business. He had read the stories suggesting that he was past his prime. He had heard fans argue that he was tiring himself out by playing every game. Now, Cal wanted to show everyone—including himself—that he was still an all-star. "I looked in the mirror and asked, 'Is my talent dwindling?' " Cal said. "I had to get rid of the doubts. So I did two things before the 1991 season. I worked harder over the winter than I ever had before. And I mentally focused on what it would take to have a great season. That was my plan."

The plan worked. In spring training, one line drive after

another flew off of Ripken's bat under the hot Florida sun. And the pounding continued when the regular season started.

In the fourth game of the year, against the Texas Rangers, Cal smacked a triple, a single, and a homer in his first four at bats. He came up in the eighth inning needing a double to hit for the cycle—which means getting each type of hit in a game. It didn't happen. Rangers' pitcher Brad Arnsberg tried to sneak a fastball past Ripken, who sent his second home run of the game sailing over the center-field wall. For the night, Cal was four-for-five, with three runs scored and a career-best seven RBIs.

It was a great night, even for Cal. But the rest of the season wasn't too much different. A year after many people thought Cal had fallen from great to just good, he had the best season of his career. He hit .323 with 46 doubles, 34 homers, and 114 RBIs. He became the first shortstop to lead his league in every fielding category: putouts, assists, chances, double plays, and fielding percentage. He won the first Gold Glove Award of his career, meaning that opposing managers felt he was the American League's best-fielding shortstop.

Not only was this the best season of Cal's career, but it was also one of the greatest all-around seasons by any shortstop in baseball history. His 34 homers made him just the fourth shortstop ever to hit more than 30 in a year. In fact, he became only the second shortstop ever to bat over .300 with 30 homers and 100 RBIs in a season. Ernie Banks of the Chicago Cubs was the first.

The numbers tell just part of the story. They don't say anything about leadership. They don't explain how important Ripken's clutch hitting is to the Orioles.

Consider, for example, a game against the Seattle Mariners in late July of 1991. It turned out to be Cal's 1,500th straight game, which earned him a standing ovation from the

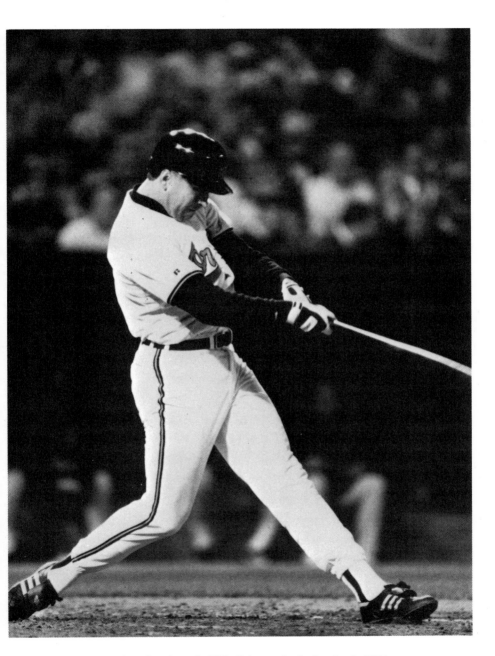

After slumping through 1990, Cal came back slugging in 1991.

Baltimore crowd. It also was the night Cal was handed his trophy as the Most Valuable Player of the 1991 All-Star game. That started another ovation.

The honors were nice. But honors don't win games. Ripken would have to do that himself. With the Orioles down 1-0 in the seventh inning, Cal came up with a runner on first. He quickly knocked Mariners' pitcher Rich DeLucia's first pitch out of the park for a home run. It won the game for the Orioles and earned Ripken his third standing ovation of the night.

"Without a doubt, this was a special night," Ripken said afterward. "I try to downplay it and not get caught up in it, but the way the fans received me, I hold this night deep."

Cal never needs to worry about how the fans feel about him. He is easily the most popular player in Baltimore and one of the most popular in baseball. His performance is one reason. The way he treats people is another.

Ripken and his wife, Kelly, helped start a program in Baltimore to teach reading to adults who never learned how. They have given hundreds of thousands of dollars to the program.

In addition, Cal spends one afternoon a week at Baltimore's stadium answering every letter he receives from fans. He has been known to hang around the ballpark for more than an hour after games, signing more than 500 autographs.

"That part goes with the job," he says. "If no one wanted to talk to you, I guess that would mean you're having a pretty bad season." It wasn't just fans who recognized Ripken's great 1991 season. So did the baseball writers who vote for the league's Most Valuable Player award. That November, they decided that Cal was the American League's top player for the second time in his career. He received 15 of the 24 first-place

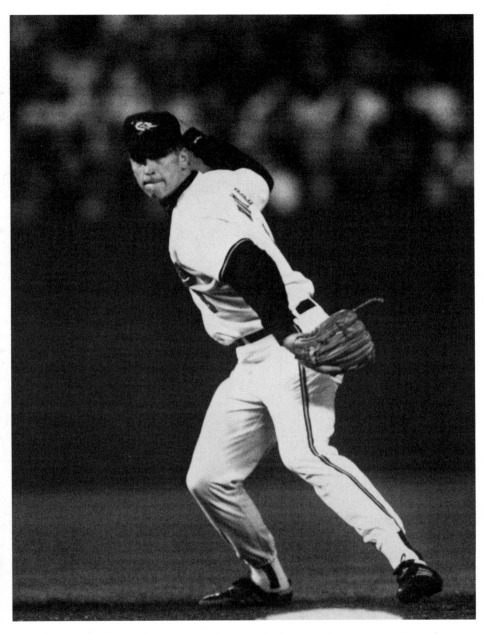

Cal is not a flashy player. Instead, he is steady and sure. There is no weakness in his game.

votes. Finishing second was the Detroit Tigers' Cecil Fielder, who had pounded out a league-best 44 home runs.

In winning the award, Ripken became the first player from a losing team to be named MVP. Despite Cal's phenomenal performance, the Orioles finished in sixth place in 1991. So it was all a mixed blessing for Ripken.

"When you're an athlete in a team sport, the only thing that really matters is winning," Ripken said after being handed the gold MVP trophy. "I appreciate this honor, but nothing beats playing in the World Series. I would trade this award for another chance to be there."

Will Ripken get another chance to play in the World Series? That's difficult to say. Baseball teams can go from bad to good in one season these days. And the Orioles certainly have some good young players. But most major leaguers consider themselves lucky to be on one championship team. Ripken is going for two.

A few days after winning the 1991 MVP award, Ripken went to a party honoring him at the Orioles' brand-new stadium. He drank milk from a champagne glass. He toasted not himself, but his teammates. He told them how he had worried just a year earlier that his career was headed downward. His return to greatness, he said, could be the start of the Orioles' return to greatness.

The Orioles did contend in 1992, and Ripken was again a key part of their success. Late in the season, he signed a five-year, $32.5 million contract that made him the best-paid player in baseball history. By the time the contract ends, Ripken may be regarded as not just a future Hall of Famer, but as one of the best players ever.

By that time, Cal will surely break Ernie Banks's record for most homers by a shortstop. He needed about 20 more for that record entering the 1993 season.

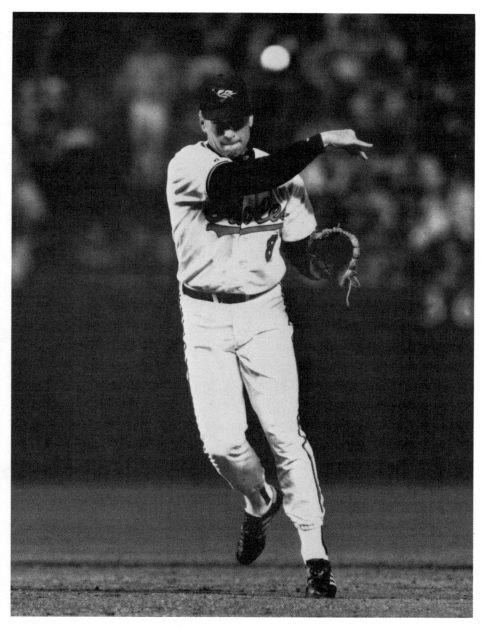

Cal may be considered the best shortstop in history. Some day, Ripken will be in the Hall of Fame.

By that time, Ripken will probably also break Joe Cronin's record of 1,424 runs batted in by an American League shortstop. He was about 375 away from that mark at the end of 1992. Cronin is regarded by most baseball experts as the best shortstop ever in the American League. You can expect that opinion to change in the next few years.

And, of course, by the time he is finished, Ripken may break Lou Gehrig's record for playing in the most games in a row. That would be his greatest achievement, especially considering that he plays the exhausting position of shortstop. In a way, Ripken has done for shortstop what basketball great Magic Johnson did for the position of point guard. He proved that a six-foot, four-inch, 220-pounder can play the position requiring the most grace, quickness, and agility. Ripken has said that he wants to be remembered as an "iron man," meaning a player who went out there and put it on the line every day. He wants people to say, "They couldn't keep Cal out of the lineup." And he wants to be recalled as a winning player.

Ripken once said, "I have talent, no doubt. My advantage is that I know the game well. The reason is that I grew up in it and had a good teacher in my father. I'm sure that whatever I am as a man and as a ballplayer comes from the way I was raised.

"But am I a superstar? Oh, no. I don't think I stack up with the great players in the league."

Anyone who has seen Cal Ripken, Jr., play knows differently.

Career Statistics

Year	Team	G	AB	R	H	2b	3b	HR	RBI	SB	AVG.
1978	Bluefield*	63	239	27	63	7	1	0	24	1	.264
1979	Miami*	105	393	51	119	28	1	5	54	4	.303
	Charlotte*	17	61	6	11	0	1	3	8	1	.180
1980	Charlotte*	144	522	91	144	28	5	25	78	4	.276
1981	Rochester*	114	437	74	126	31	4	23	75	0	.288
	Orioles	23	39	1	5	0	0	0	0	0	.128
1982	Orioles	160	598	90	158	32	5	28	93	3	.264
1983	Orioles	162	663	121	211	47	2	27	102	0	.318
1984	Orioles	162	641	103	195	37	7	27	86	2	.304
1985	Orioles	161	642	116	181	32	5	26	110	2	.282
1986	Orioles	162	627	98	177	35	1	25	81	4	.282
1987	Orioles	162	624	97	157	28	3	27	98	3	.252
1988	Orioles	161	575	87	152	25	1	23	81	2	.264
1989	Orioles	162	646	80	166	30	0	21	93	3	.257
1990	Orioles	161	600	78	150	28	4	21	84	3	.250
1991	Orioles	162	650	99	210	46	5	34	114	6	.323
Major League Totals		1638	6350	970	1762	340	33	259	942	28	.279

*Minor Leagues

61

Where to Write Cal Ripken, Jr.:

Mr. Cal Ripken, Jr.
c/o Baltimore Orioles
Orioles Park at Camden Yards
333 West Camden Street
Baltimore, MD 21201

Index